The Children's Republic

Also by Hannah Moscovitch

Bunny
East of Berlin
Infinity (with Njo Kong Kie)
Little One and Other Plays
The Mill Part Two: The Huron Bride
Post-Democracy
The Russian Play and Other Short Works
Secret Life of a Mother (with Maev Beaty and Ann-Marie Kerr)
Sexual Misconduct of the Middle Classes
This is War
What a Young Wife Ought to Know

The Children's Republic

a play about Janusz Korczak

Hannah Moscovitch

Playwrights Canada Press
Toronto

For professional or amateur production rights, please contact:
Ian Arnold at Catalyst TCM
15 Old Primrose Lane, Toronto, ON M5A 4T1
416-568-8673 | ian@catalysttcm.com

LIBRARY AND ARCHIVES CANADA CATALOGUING IN PUBLICATION
Title: The children's republic / Hannah Moscovitch.
Names: Moscovitch, Hannah, author.
Description: First edition. | A play.
Identifiers: Canadiana (print) 20200375814 | Canadiana (ebook) 20200375822
  | ISBN 9780369101457 (softcover) | ISBN 9780369101464 (PDF)
  | ISBN 9780369101471 (EPUB) | ISBN 9780369101488 (Kindle)
Subjects: LCSH: Korczak, Janusz, 1878-1942—Drama.
Classification: LCC PS8626.0837 C45 2020 | DDC C812/.6—dc23

Playwrights Canada Press operates on land which is the ancestral home of the Anishinaabe Nations (Ojibwe / Chippewa, Odawa, Potawatomi, Algonquin, Saulteaux, Nipissing, and Mississauga), the Wendat, and the members of the Haudenosaunee Confederacy (Mohawk, Oneida, Onondaga, Cayuga, Seneca, and Tuscarora), as well as Metis and Inuit peoples. It always was and always will be Indigenous land.

We acknowledge the financial support of the Canada Council for the Arts—which last year invested $153 million to bring the arts to Canadians throughout the country—the Ontario Arts Council (OAC), Ontario Creates, and the Government of Canada for our publishing activities.

 Canada Council Conseil des arts
for the Arts du Canada

 ONTARIO ARTS COUNCIL
CONSEIL DES ARTS DE L'ONTARIO
an Ontario government agency
un organisme du gouvernement de l'Ontario

 Canada ONTARIO CREATES | ONTARIO CRÉATIF

To the children who performed this play.

Foreword
Stephanie Levitz

Today, when girls like Malala Yousafzai and Greta Thunberg become global activists for education, for climate change, for racial and social justice, their voices are celebrated and encouraged by the adults around them. But over one hundred years ago, a Polish physician and educator often found himself sidelined for suggesting children shouldn't just speak up—it was their right to do so. Still, Janusz Korczak persisted. His work on theories of child development to incorporate the importances of the rights of children would eventually inspire a landmark international treaty: the United Nations Convention on the Rights of the Child.

His work wasn't only theoretical. In 1912, Korczak set up an orphanage for Jewish children in Warsaw where hundreds of boys and girls whose parents were too destitute to care for them, or had died, were under his care. He ran his orphanage as if his charges were citizens of a country—a children's republic. Their rights were clearly laid out in a charter. Rule-breakers faced trial by a jury of their peers. Achievements—even things as simple as getting up on time for a certain number of days in a row—were celebrated, to give the children a sense of accomplishment. And when a child left, most often in those days to be sent abroad to family, those who remained took a vote to determine how they felt.

My grandfather, Leon Gluzman, who entered the orphanage at the age of six, received one hundred votes regretting his departure, four in favour, and sixteen abstentions. My grandfather was on his way to Canada to live with extended family. The year was 1929, the Second World War had yet to break out, and the vicious anti-Semitism that would eventually lead to the Holocaust was only just beginning to take hold. He kept in touch with Korczak until 1939. In 1941, with war now raging, he received an urgent plea from the man many called "the old doctor," asking for care packages to help the ailing orphans. A year later, with the Nazis in full control, most of the Jews of Warsaw were rounded up—Korzcak and his children among them. Though he held a position of prominence in Polish society and was offered a way to safety, Korzcak would not leave the children. He marched with them onto a train that was headed for the notorious death camp of Treblinka. He and all the children in his care were killed. Altogether, six million Jews were killed in the Holocaust, members of my grandfather's family among them.

As he built a life in Ottawa, my grandfather spoke infrequently of what happened to his family left behind in Europe. Nor did he share his connection to Korczak, though the story of the orphanage and its tragic end were becoming known throughout the world. He became an accountant, and with his wife Ann raised four children, and later was the proud zaidie—grandfather—of nine.

While he didn't speak much of his Korczak connection, he did live his values. One reason we were so close when I was a child was that unlike many adults, my grandfather always treated me as an equal and listened carefully to what I had to say. Like Korczak also, my grandfather believed that education ought to be well-rounded. He was a patron of the Ottawa School of Speech and Drama, a tenant in one of the buildings he owned.

Upon hearing his story, director Amanda Lewis declared that it ought to be turned into a play to honour his support for the school. Hannah Moscovitch was commissioned to write one, and *The Children's Republic* premiered in 2009.

My grandfather died in 2012. He wasn't a religious man, but this publication of the play fulfils a value of his faith, one important to him and to our family: the importance of sharing wisdom and guidance from one generation to the next. May those who read, perform in, or watch this play also be inspired to share its lessons: the value of an education, of kindness, and the right of every child to have a voice.

Stephanie Levitz is an award-winning political affairs journalist with the Canadian Press, Canada's national newswire agency. Over the last two decades, her work has taken her around the country and the world, covering events including federal elections, G7, G20, and other international summits, the Beijing and Vancouver Olympics, and the war in Afghanistan. She is also a regular guest on nationally televised programs including CTV's Question Period. *She is a graduate of McGill University and Columbia University's School of Journalism. She lives in Ottawa with her husband and two children, around the corner from her grandfather Leon's longtime Ottawa home.*

The Children's Republic was commissioned, developed, and first produced by the Great Canadian Theatre Company and the Ottawa School of Speech and Drama at the Great Canadian Theatre Company, Ottawa, from November 3 to November 22, 2009, with the following cast and creative team:

Starring Peter Froehlich, Kate Hurman, Hannah Kaya, Juliana Krajcovic, Luke Letourneau, Sarah McVie, Leah Morris, Adrien Pyke, Paul Rainville, and Louis Sobol

Director: Janet Irwin
Set and Costume Design: Camellia Koo
Lighting Design: Jock Munro
Live Composer and Musical Director: Nick Carpenter
Recorded Composer and Sound Designer: Marc Desormeaux
Movement Director: Peter Ryan
Fight Director: John Koensgen
Stage Manager: Kevin Waghorn
Apprentice Stage Manager: Louisa Haché
Assistant Director: Patrick Gauthier
Child Minder: Lindsay Carkner
Creative Producer, Ottawa School of Speech and Drama: Amanda Lewis
Dramaturg: Lise Ann Johnson

The play was later substantially redrafted and produced by the Harold Green Jewish Theatre Company and the Tarragon Theatre at the Tarragon Theatre Mainspace, Toronto, from November 8 to December 18, 2011, with the following cast and creative team:

Starring Emma Burke-Kleinman, Katie Frances Cohen, Mark Correia, Peter Hutt, Kelli Fox, Elliot Larson, and Amy Rutherford

Director: Alisa Palmer
Costume Design: Camellia Koo
Lighting Design: Kimberly Purtell
Sound Design: John Gzowski
Fight Director: John Stead
Stage Manager: Diane Konkin
Apprentice Stage Manager: Meghan Speakman
Assistant Director: Kristina Nicoll
Script Coordinator: Nicholas Hutcheson

The play was again redrafted with commission from and then produced by the Belfry Theatre, Victoria, from September 12 to October 8, 2017, with the following cast and creative team:

Starring Lily Cave, Sophia Irene Coopman, Zander Eke, Paul Rainville, Kerry Sandomirsky, Simeon Sanford Blades, and Sari Alesh

Director: Christian Barry
Designer: Camellia Koo
Lighting Design: Kaitlin Hickey
Stage Manager: Jennifer Swan
Assistant Stage Manager: Sadie Fox

If a child has a life where cruelty has become the norm, what a powerful effect would be the memory of that person—perhaps the only one—who showed kindness, understanding, and respect. The child's future life and sense of his self could take a different course, knowing there was one person who would not fail him.
—Janusz Korczak, *Loving Every Child*

The soul of a child is as complicated as ours and as full of contradictions. A teacher who, instead of enforcing, emancipates, who does not pull but raises up, does not oppress but molds, does not dictate but instructs, does not demand but asks, is destined to live through many inspired moments with the child and will frequently be able to observe, through a veil of tears, the struggle between good and evil forces, and to watch the white angel walk off with the trump card.
—Janusz Korczak

Characters

Israel—early teens
Misha—late childhood to early teens
Mettye—late childhood to early teens
Sara—late childhood to early teens
Janusz Korczak—sixties
Stefa Wilczynska—forties to fifties

Notes

Doctor Janusz Korczak and Stefa Wilczynska are historical figures. Israel, Misha, Mettye, and Sara are the creation of the author, loosely inspired by accounts of Korczak's wards.

Young performers should play the roles for young people. The young performers play both their characters and the narrators of the piece.

A beat indicates one musical beat. A pause indicates three musical beats.

Stage directions in this draft are meant to reflect what occurred during the Belfry Theatre production of the play.

Other than a large chalkboard and microphones, the stage starts empty. There are no large set pieces. Props, costumes, and small set pieces are only brought on, off, and moved by the young performers. The young performers also control onstage lowlights. They control the stage.

In our production, a professional violinist was hired to play the part of Sara's violin. Sara's violin was abstracted. Violin music was also used throughout as the soundscape, and in particular during transitions.

Act One

Prologue.

The violinist plays.

The YOUNG PERFORMERS *gaze out at the audience. Then they turn and write the following words onto the set with chalk:*

1940
400,000 Jews sealed in with brick walls and barbed wire
The Warsaw Ghetto

They draw barbed wire on the walls as well. Then they turn and look out at the audience again, regarding us in the gloom.

Transition.

Intermezzo One.

We hear a violin playing very faintly, off.

The PERFORMER PLAYING MISHA approaches the audience and speaks into a microphone.

PERFORMER PLAYING MISHA: *(to audience)* The Warsaw Ghetto. Gesia Street. The wind blows. There's one working street light.

A dim light comes on, illuminating KORCZAK.

Someone, somewhere is playing the violin.

Beat.

The doctor's on his way back to the Orphan's Home.

KORCZAK checks his watch.

It's three minutes to curfew.

KORCZAK sees ISRAEL.

Transition.

Scene One.

KORCZAK approaches ISRAEL, who is sitting on the ground and crying.

KORCZAK: It's almost curfew—

ISRAEL sees him, turns away, and tries to stop crying.

Do you have somewhere to go?

ISRAEL: My . . . father—I lost his . . . money—I . . . lost it, I don't know where, and the street's dark. It was . . . for bread . . . and I don't . . . want to . . . go home and—

KORCZAK: How much?

ISRAEL: Ten groszy.

KORCZAK takes out his wallet and counts the coins out. ISRAEL watches KORCZAK, his breathing still jagged.

KORCZAK: Ten. Ten groszy . . . can buy you what? A piece of bread? How often have you used that trick before?

ISRAEL stops crying, goes still, and looks at KORCZAK, watchful.

It's a good trick: you cry very well. And now I have my wallet out, and the street's dark, and I'm old and feeble . . .

> ISRAEL, *his face blank, stands up quickly and moves toward* KORCZAK. KORCZAK *steps back.*

Don't . . . don't . . . Take it.

> KORCZAK *holds out his wallet.* ISRAEL *takes another step forward, reaches out, and slowly, menacingly, takes the wallet out of* KORCZAK'S *hands.* ISRAEL *turns and walks away.*

(calls to him) Are you hungry?

> ISRAEL *stops, looks back at him, wary.*

You look it. What do you do after curfew? You hide, or . . . They shoot at you? They've shot at you? Where's your father: Is he dead? Your mother too?

> ISRAEL *turns and walks away again.*

You have a little money there, but would you like some soup? The kitchen makes it from leftovers. Sometimes it's good and sometimes it's . . . hot. You know these streets?

ISRAEL: Yeah?

KORCZAK: It's over on Chlodna. Number thirty-three. There's a bed for you, too, if you want to . . . get inside after curfew.

> *Beat.*

What's your name?

ISRAEL: Israel.

KORCZAK: Israel, your father's dead.

ISRAEL hesitates, looks at him, holding the wallet.

Transition.

Scene Two.

We're in a lecture hall. KORCZAK *regards and then speaks to the audience as though they are his lecture audience.* MISHA *is in the background.*

KORCZAK: Thank you to the Bund for hosting this lecture series. It's nice to give a talk: be reminded of my old life, be reminded that the war will end, and we'll put thought into how to raise a good child, a smart child, a strong child again.

KORCZAK smiles. He thinks for a moment.

When I was young, I worked at the Bersohn and Bauman Hospital, treating children from the poor districts. The children, they often weren't sick, they were . . . malnourished, and I don't mean only physically—although it's true you can't live on potatoes and tea alone—the children were . . . morally malnourished—they were lonely and stupid and they knew it, and they were ashamed of it. I treated children for minor ailments, rickets or fever, and then I sent them back out again into the streets where no light reached them, and where their wretchedness and stupidity had no meaning. These young citizens of tomorrow . . . But children, I felt, were people *today*, not tomorrow, so I founded the orphanage. That way, I could treat the whole child, the soul. I was told then by the director of the hospital that "the soul is the purview of the divine," and "reformers always come to a bad end."

KORCZAK smiles.

Well. But this is talk. Misha.

> *MISHA steps forward and stands beside KORCZAK.*

(to audience) This is Misha. And this is what I can teach you about pedagogy.

(to MISHA) Will you hold this microphone up against your chest?

> *KORCZAK hands MISHA a microphone.*

> *MISHA holds the microphone up against his chest.*

(to MISHA, low) Thank you.

> *The sound of a heart pounding fills the auditorium.*

(to audience) This is how a child's heart sounds in the presence of adults.

> *MISHA's face is blank.*

> *But MISHA's heart is pounding as he looks out at us.*

> *The sound of his heart echoes in the lecture hall.*

> *This goes on for ten to twenty seconds.*

> *KORCZAK takes the microphone back from MISHA.*

Everything else is commentary.

> *Blackout.*

Scene Three.

We're in the boys' dormitory.

KORCZAK, METTYE, and ISRAEL stand blinking in the relative darkness, under a light bulb. KORCZAK holds the chain to the light bulb. METTYE stands close to KORCZAK, and STEFA and MISHA stand nearer to the door. They're all watching for ISRAEL's reaction.

KORCZAK: *(to ISRAEL)* It's not what you're used to: it's a big room . . . ?

Pause. ISRAEL is impassive, blank.

STEFA looks at her pocket watch.

STEFA: *(to KORCZAK)* Janusz.

KORCZAK: Mm?

STEFA: It's six.

KORCZAK: Ah. But, Stefa, is it all right if I talk a little?

STEFA: No.

KORCZAK: Please: to welcome him.

STEFA: No.

KORCZAK: *(to MISHA)* Misha, ask Stefa if I can talk a little.

STEFA: *(to KORCZAK)* No.

MISHA: *(to STEFA)* The doctor wants to talk a little.

STEFA: *(to KORCZAK)* Tell him it's dinnertime and he never "talks a little."

ISRAEL: *(to KORCZAK)* We sleep here?

KORCZAK: Yes: sleep at night, study in the day.

ISRAEL: How many.

KORCZAK: *(to ISRAEL)* Half of you. Ninety-six boys. The girls are—

STEFA: Janusz.

KORCZAK: Mm?

STEFA: It's dinner.

KORCZAK: You go: take Misha and Mettye.

(off STEFA's look) We have a new ward: I can't talk to him for two minutes?

STEFA: Two minutes. Two minutes he says!

KORCZAK: Two minutes!

STEFA calls to METTYE, who is standing too close to KORCZAK, and MISHA.

STEFA: Misha—Mettye, go, go.

METTYE: *(to KORCZAK, hanging off of him)* Doctor? My bird's up on the roof in its cage and, Doctor: I think it likes its cage—

STEFA: Mettye.

METTYE: I think it wants to stay in its cage—

STEFA: *(to METTYE)* Mettye! What did I say?

STEFA exits with MISHA and METTYE.

Beat. ISRAEL looks at the dormitory.

KORCZAK: *(of the room)* What does it look like to you?

Beat.

Like a hospital?

Beat.

Like a prison?

Beat.

Like a morgue?

ISRAEL: A . . . what?

KORCZAK: Where the dead are kept.

ISRAEL: That's a graveyard.

ISRAEL turns and looks at the room.

KORCZAK: Oh, a graveyard. That's what it looks like to you . . . ? The cots are the graves . . . ?

ISRAEL turns and walks toward the door.

Israel?

ISRAEL: *(exiting)* I'll sleep here.

KORCZAK: No, wait—Israel.

KORCZAK catches up and goes to put his hand on ISRAEL.

ISRAEL flinches away as though he's expecting to be hit.

KORCZAK backs up.

(a statement) I'm not going to hit you.

ISRAEL unclenches and looks at KORCZAK.

(gently) What happened in the graveyard?

Beat.

If you don't want to sleep in here you can stay in the infirmary.

ISRAEL: I'll—no—I'll sleep here.

Transition.

Intermezzo Two.

The PERFORMER PLAYING MISHA *enters.*

PERFORMER PLAYING MISHA: *(to audience)* A corridor in the ghetto orphanage. Stefa and the doctor talk every night in this corridor. Stefa arrives first, as usual.

STEFA enters.

She has something important to talk to the doctor about, something she knows the doctor won't like.

In response to MISHA's *speech to the audience,* STEFA *raps her pen against her notepad, agitated.*

And here comes the doctor. Two minutes late, as usual.

KORCZAK enters, hurrying, huffing, and holding his pocket watch.

Transition.

Scene Four.

STEFA and KORCZAK stand in a hallway and confer. During the scene, STEFA consults her notebook.

KORCZAK: I'm sorry I'm late: I was talking to Mettye about her bird—

STEFA clicks her tongue.

Oh the clicking, the infamous disapproving clicking of Stefa Wilczynska: click, click, click.

Beat.

(off STEFA's look, sincere now) I'm late, again. I'm sorry. Go ahead—

STEFA: Three things. Tomorrow, go to the council, to Altman, he should have a shipment of bread for you.

KORCZAK: Yes. And?

STEFA: Misha. I found a pile of rotting bread in his bed. He's smuggling it during meals and hiding it under his mattress. It's going to attract rats.

KORCZAK: *(nodding)* I'll talk to him.

STEFA: And . . . Israel—

KORCZAK: Ah! Here we go: Israel.

STEFA: He didn't sleep in his bed: we found him lying underneath it—

KORCZAK: So he lies under his bed? So what?

STEFA: And—I'm not finished!

KORCZAK: Mettye's mother left her so she clings to her bird: Israel's been in the streets, in the ghetto, so he—

STEFA: —*and this morning* he cracked the urinal in the boy's wash-room. Urine all over the floor, and all the boys stepping in it: urine in the corridor, urine on the stairs, urine in the dining room, urine / in the kitchen—

KORCZAK: *(off STEFA's look, rubbing his eyes)* All right, Stefa, urine! A lot of urine! So, yes, so I'll talk to him—

STEFA: No, this one's different—

KORCZAK: *(under / simultaneous to STEFA's line)* You're forgetting—

STEFA: No I'm not—

KORCZAK: —how difficult some of them / have been—

STEFA: —this one's—no, I'm not—this one's—no. I don't like him: I don't like how he looks at the other children.

KORCZAK: You don't like how he . . . How does he look at / them?

STEFA: He's not even a child, he's—

KORCZAK: Then what is he?

STEFA: He's—I doubt he knows his age, but he's not a child, and you think he's going to sit and study tomorrow? He's going to *break something.*

Beat.

KORCZAK: So what? What do I do with him? I walk him back out to the streets—?

STEFA: No, you take him to one of the other orphanages: / the one on Dzielna . . .

KORCZAK: I say, "You broke our urinal and Stefa doesn't like how you look at the other children and good luck with the Nazis."

STEFA: Janusz.

KORCZAK: What?

STEFA: Janusz.

KORCZAK: What—*what?* In that tone: "Janusz." I'm not being difficult—

STEFA: Janusz.

KORCZAK: I'm not! Someone has to look after children like him.

STEFA: Oh good: ideals—

KORCZAK: There'll be more like him. They'll grow up stepping over bodies, and then the war'll end and what'll they be like?

Beat. A stand-off.

STEFA: Fine. Fine. It's your funeral.

KORCZAK: If it's my funeral then *Israel is invited to my funeral!*

STEFA: *(without looking up)* Fine.

KORCZAK: Fine! Fine!

STEFA is walking away. KORCZAK turns and walks away.

(to himself) Fine!

Transition.

Intermezzo Three.

The PERFORMER PLAYING METTYE comes on stage, takes STEFA by the hand, and walks her to the front of the stage. The PERFORMER PLAYING METTYE speaks into a microphone.

PERFORMER PLAYING METTYE: *(to audience)* Stefa's the manager of the Orphan's Home. She's been working with the doctor since 1912. Twenty-nine years.

The PERFORMER PLAYING METTYE looks at STEFA. STEFA's face has soured.

A long time.

Transition.

Scene Five.

METTYE practises her Hebrew letters on a chalkboard. MISHA sits with books. STEFA and ISRAEL talk.

STEFA: Have you been in school?

ISRAEL: No.

STEFA: Can you do any mathematics?

ISRAEL: Some.

STEFA: Like what?

ISRAEL shrugs.

ISRAEL: Money.

STEFA: Can you read . . . ?

ISRAEL looks at her.

No?

ISRAEL looks at her.

And you're how old . . . ?

> *Beat. They eye each other.*

I have crooked teeth, and three moles on my cheeks, and one bad child liked to tell me I looked like a bun with raisins in it. I'm a plain-looking woman. I have been my whole life: so you go ahead and take a good long look and you say the worst thing you can think of.

> *ISRAEL looks away, angry.*

Well, I don't know what to do for you. I suppose you could draw.

> *STEFA goes and gets ISRAEL a couple of stubs of pencils (including a red one) and a sheet of paper.*

Draw on the paper *only.*

> *ISRAEL shrugs to himself and sits down and draws. STEFA goes out. Once the adult supervision is gone, METTYE fixes on ISRAEL, comes over, and sits very near to him.*

> *ISRAEL doesn't look up from his paper or acknowledge METTYE in any way. METTYE sings the following song directly to ISRAEL:*

METTYE: *(singing)* Don't you cry for food, your mother's gone to get you some.
When she comes back, she'll give you
Butter from a bowl.
Sausage from a spoon.
Crumbs from a cup.
When she comes back, she'll give you nothing instead.
Then rip off your head.
And frrr straight to Warsaw she'll fly.
Before she goes back to the sky.

Beat.

(to ISRAEL*)* Do you like my singing?

    ISRAEL *doesn't respond.* METTYE *starts again.*

(singing) Don't you cry for food, your mother's gone to get you some.
When she comes back, she'll give you
Soup in a bowl.
Soup in a bowl.
Soup in a bowl.
Soup in a bowl.
Soup in a bowl.
Soup in a bowl,
Soup in a bowl,
Soup in a—

    ISRAEL *looks at her.*

    Beat. METTYE *freezes and shrinks back from him.* ISRAEL *goes back*
    to drawing.

—bowl.
Soup in a bowl.
Soup in a bowl.
Soup in a bowl.
Soup in a bowl—

    STEFA *has walked back in to check on them.*

STEFA: Mettye! Get away from him.

    METTYE *goes back to the blackboard and tracing letters.* ISRAEL
    covers up what he's been drawing. STEFA *clocks it.*

What? I can't see what you're drawing?

ISRAEL looks at her.

Why not?

Beat.

Is it a drawing of me?

STEFA holds out her hand.

Beat. A standoff.

Give it to me.

ISRAEL: It's not you.

STEFA: Good, fine: then there's no reason not to show it to me.

Beat.

ISRAEL: No.

STEFA grabs the paper. She looks at it for a suspended moment. And then rips it up.

STEFA: Sit there and do nothing then.

STEFA goes out. ISRAEL looks down at the torn pieces of paper.

Meanwhile METTYE is gazing at ISRAEL, getting ready to harass him again.

METTYE: *(to ISRAEL)* You've got lice in your hair.

MISHA: Mettye.

METTYE: What?

MISHA: No he doesn't.

METTYE: *(to MISHA)* He does.

(to ISRAEL) You should go to the infirmary and ask for lice powder—

MISHA: *(to METTYE)* He doesn't have lice.

METTYE: *to MISHA)* He does! I can see them from here. Either that or his hair's very dirty—

MISHA: *(to METTYE) Shut up.*

> *Beat. But METTYE can't resist.*

METTYE: *(to ISRAEL, direct)* You've got lice.

> *ISRAEL turns and looks at METTYE.*

(off ISRAEL) No, no, no, no, no . . .

> *We suspend for a moment. There's a drone on the violin. The*
> *PERFORMER PLAYING MISHA turns and speaks into a microphone.*

PERFORMER PLAYING MISHA: *(to audience)* Israel grabs Mettye by the hair. This is the sound she makes when her face hits the floor:

> *ISRAEL slams METTYE's face into the ground: this is abstracted.*

METTYE: *(from the impact)* Ughhhh.

> *Transition.*

Intermezzo Four.

As the stage shifts, the PERFORMER PLAYING MISHA *continues to speak to the audience.* KORCZAK *is writing in his office.*

PERFORMER PLAYING MISHA: *(to audience)* The doctor's in his office. This morning, in the ghetto, he saw a thirteen-year-old girl hanged for smuggling.

KORCZAK looks up, fights down a wave of emotion.

He stayed until her legs stopped moving.

With some effort KORCZAK *forces himself to continue to write.*

Transition.

Scene Six.

STEFA comes into KORCZAK's office.

STEFA: Korczak?

KORCZAK: Mm?

STEFA: You're writing.

KORCZAK: As you can see.

STEFA: Two things. First, there's a child we should consider for the orphanage.

KORCZAK: Why?

STEFA: She's a prodigy.

KORCZAK: A prodigy. Just generally a prodigy?

STEFA: She plays the violin.

KORCZAK: Violin! A violin prodigy: seems a little extravagant for a decrepit old orphanage on Chlodna Street. Do we need a prodigy? Do we deserve a prodigy?

STEFA: She can play at our patron salons.

    Beat.

You like music.

KORCZAK: Her parents are dead?

STEFA: They were shot.

    Finally KORCZAK turns and looks at STEFA.

They were taken out in front of their apartment building and shot. The neighbours found her sitting with their bodies.

KORCZAK: Why were they shot?

STEFA: Who knows.

    Beat.

KORCZAK: Yes to the violin prodigy!

STEFA: Two: Israel got in a fight with Mettye.

    KORCZAK looks up again.

KORCZAK: Ah.

STEFA: She's in the infirmary. He's out in the hallway. I'll send him in?

KORCZAK: Yes.

STEFA: Her nose is broken.

KORCZAK: I'll talk to him—

STEFA slams her notebook shut with a bang. KORCZAK looks up at her.

STEFA: He broke her nose.

KORCZAK: All right, Stefa.

STEFA goes out. ISRAEL appears in the doorway. KORCZAK observes him. There's blood on his hands and his shirt, and on a handker- chief he's wiping his hands with.

She bled a lot.

ISRAEL: Yeah.

KORCZAK: Come in.

ISRAEL steps inside KORCZAK's office and sits down in the chair in front of him.

A lot of the children here were malnourished when they were little. Misha, for example. He had rickets, so his bones are weak and . . . fragile: like chalk. And the kind of fighting you know . . . !

ISRAEL: Like chalk?

KORCZAK: Yes.

Beat.

I'd rather you break the urinals than the children. I'd rather you don't break the urinals, either, but . . . for now . . . the chairs, the walls . . . the sinks?

Beat.

What happened: you were . . . sitting with the other children and . . . Did someone—did Mettye—say something to you? Something you didn't like . . . ?

ISRAEL looks at him.

You're cold. Here.

KORCZAK goes to take ISRAEL's hands. ISRAEL flinches back—and KORCZAK warms them in his. ISRAEL, despite himself and though it's unfamiliar to him, likes the contact. Is mesmerized by it.

It's cold for this time of year, hm? Mettye is a nudge, but she only nudges people she likes. It's how she shows her interest in a person, her affection for them. But you: you don't like her?

ISRAEL shrugs.

Or, you do like her.

ISRAEL shrugs.

A shrug for "you don't like her" and a shrug for "you do like her." You should go visit her in the infirmary. Bring her a small thing: a shiny pebble or a pine cone. She'll like that.

Beat. ISRAEL eyes KORCZAK warily.

Stefa's said that you're not sleeping well.

ISRAEL shrugs.

I . . . write, at night, in my office. If you'd rather not lie there, awake, by yourself, come sit with me.

Beat.

What?

ISRAEL: That's it?

KORCZAK: Oh, Mettye? You'll go on trial for breaking her nose, at the Children's Court, but no, I don't punish you.

ISRAEL watches KORCZAK rub his hands a few seconds longer.

Then he pulls his hands away.

ISRAEL: I'll go then?

Transition.

Scene Seven.

METTYE and SARA are in the orphanage infirmary, in cots (in our production the cots were abstracted to a blanket and a rectangle of light). SARA holds her violin wrapped in a scarf. Bored, METTYE looks around the infirmary for something to do. She fixes on SARA for a moment, then:

METTYE: You're new? Hey, you're new? You're new?

Beat.

I have a bird in a cage, up on the roof: the doctor gave it to me. I could show it to you.

Beat.

You're new.

Beat.

YOU'RE? NEW? HEY YOU'RE . . . NEW!!!!

Beat.

Are you dead?

SARA opens her eyes, sits up, and looks at METTYE . . .

Oh, I thought maybe you'd . . . ! What's wrong with you? Why're they keeping you in here: are you sick . . . ?

Beat.

I'm not sick: I got smacked against the floor. It was worse yesterday. The swelling's almost gone now, but Stefa says I have to lie here until my bones set. But you're sick? You're sick? Hey, you're sick? Why don't you talk? Why. Don't. You. Talk?! Are you stupid? ARE YOU STUPID AHHHH!!!!!! AHHHHHHH!!!!!

METTYE realizes.

Oh, did you—you lost your family? You did, didn't you? Did they die? Mine—my mother—she didn't die: she left, and they brought me here, well to our old building, and I was in the infirmary too because I'd been in our room, waiting for my mother to come back, with no food.

METTYE freezes because ISRAEL *has appeared in the doorway.*

ISRAEL slowly steps into the room.

(to ISRAEL*)* This is the infirmary.

ISRAEL: Yeah.

METTYE: Does Stefa know you're in here?

Beat.

Why're you in here?

ISRAEL holds a piece of ribbon out toward her.

ISRAEL: It's for you.

METTYE: It . . . is?

ISRAEL: Yeah?

METTYE: Why?

>ISRAEL *shrugs.*

>ISRAEL *puts the ribbon into* METTYE's *hand.* METTYE *cringes back but takes the gift.*

That's . . . nice?

ISRAEL: Yeah?

METTYE: It's a ribbon, for my hair?

>ISRAEL *nods.*

>*Beat. Awkward.*

Are you going to hit me again?

ISRAEL: *(re: her face)* Does it hurt?

METTYE: It did hurt, yeah!

>*Beat.*

You have lice. I'm joking! I'm joking with you: don't hit me again.

>ISRAEL *glances around the room, and then at* SARA.

She's new.

ISRAEL: Yeah?

> *ISRAEL walks over and looks at her, assesses her. ISRAEL takes a step closer, right up to SARA's bed.*

She's got a violin.

> *ISRAEL goes up to SARA and takes the violin out of her hands.*

METTYE: Don't do that.

> *SARA looks up at ISRAEL, helplessly.*

(re: the violin) Give her that back.

ISRAEL: *(a statement)* You might as well take it.

METTYE: Why?

> *METTYE takes the violin back from ISRAEL and looks at him.*

Why?

ISRAEL: *(a statement)* She's dying.

> *Beat.*

(off METTYE's look) She looks like the people that die look.

> *Beat.*

I'll go then?

*ISRAEL goes out of the infirmary. METTYE hands the violin back
to SARA.*

METTYE: *(very gentle)* No you don't: you don't look dead, and don't be
scared, it's all right.

METTYE puts her arms around SARA.

Poor thing, all alone—I'm here, I'm here now. I'll love you: it's all right.

Transition.

Intermezzo Five.

The PERFORMER PLAYING METTYE speaks into a microphone.
Meanwhile, KORCZAK writes in his office.

PERFORMER PLAYING METTYE: *(to audience)* It's evening. The doctor's writing in his office.

KORCZAK crosses out his writing: we hear his pen vigorously striking through his work. He pulls a bottle of vodka out, pours himself a glass.

It's not going very well.

KORCZAK drinks the vodka.

Transition.

Scene Eight.

KORCZAK's office at the orphanage. KORCZAK senses someone is hovering in the doorway and looks up.

KORCZAK: Misha.

MISHA: You're working.

KORCZAK: No, no, please, it's not . . . going very well: I'm happy to see you.

MISHA: I finished your manuscript.

KORCZAK: You did! Well, good. Did you like it?

MISHA: I . . . don't know. Yes, I liked it. But of course you can't actually travel to the sun, can you?

KORCZAK: No.

MISHA: So then the sun is meant to stand in for something?

KORCZAK: It is, yes.

MISHA: Like a metaphor? Or an allegory?

KORCZAK: Yes.

MISHA: For what?

KORCZAK: Your father was a scholar, isn't that right? He studied Torah? That's who you take after?

MISHA: I don't know. I don't remember him.

KORCZAK: He died when you were . . . ?

MISHA: Four.

KORCZAK: And your mother was already dead, and . . . your grand-mother took you? And . . . she didn't feed you, is that right?

MISHA shrugs.

MISHA: She fed my brother. He was older than me. Then he died, and there was more food.

KORCZAK: *(low)* Misha.

Beat.

Are you frightened? That we'll run out of food?

Beat.

Why?

MISHA: There's a war. The Germans don't like us.

KORCZAK: No, they don't.

MISHA: So if there's even less food, who will they stop feeding?

STEFA enters quickly.

STEFA: I'm sorry: I need to speak to the doctor.

(to KORCZAK) It can't wait.

MISHA waits while KORCZAK and STEFA confer in lowered voices downstage, so that MISHA can't hear.

Two things. One, I can't get Sara to eat. I'm going to bring her in for you to examine her.

KORCZAK: Our violin prodigy! And?

STEFA: My locket was stolen. Out of the locked drawer in my office. It was my mother's.

KORCZAK: Oh. Well. Hm.

STEFA: She's dead.

KORCZAK: Yes, I know! I remember that your mother's dead, Stefa! Well, we'll have to get it back.

STEFA: We will.

KORCZAK: And, what? You think Israel took it? There are other children in here that could have taken it!

STEFA: Your shirt's missing a button.

KORCZAK: What? You think he stole that too?

STEFA: Well give it to me.

KORCZAK: What? Now?

STEFA: No, no, wait until all the buttons fall off.

KORCZAK: Fine. Fine.

KORCZAK takes it off and hands it to her.

STEFA: I'll go get Sara.

KORCZAK turns back to MISHA.

He takes an apple out of his pocket puts it in both of MISHA's hands, then holds MISHA's hands in his.

KORCZAK: Misha, I'm always going to feed you. I'll worry about the war, and Germans, and food shortages: you don't need to—

MISHA: *(with some surprise)* It's an apple.

STEFA brings a very bundled up SARA into KORCZAK's office.

KORCZAK: Ah, Sara, Saraleh! I'm the old doctor. We met when you arrived.

KORCZAK takes his stethoscope out and goes over to SARA, gently pressing it against her chest. SARA is very blank and dazed. Meanwhile, MISHA gets up and goes toward the door.

(to MISHA) Misha? You're driving Stefa crazy with your bread under the mattress—

MISHA: Oh!

KORCZAK: So no more bread under the mattress.

MISHA: *(to STEFA)* Sorry, Stefa.

He goes out. KORCZAK turns to SARA.

KORCZAK: *(to SARA)* I'm going to put my finger on your wrist, like this, so I can listen to your heart beating.

KORCZAK puts his thumb on her wrist.

STEFA: She won't eat soup. She won't eat bread soaked in milk. She won't even drink a cup of tea.

KORCZAK: *(to SARA)* You have to eat, Sara, or Stefa's head will burst open. I've seen it happen before. All her brains fall out onto the floor. Phhfffff!

SARA looks up at him, unsmiling, numb.

KORCZAK looks at his pocket watch.

STEFA: Her pulse?

KORCZAK: *(to STEFA)* Her pulse is slow.

(to SARA) And you find you can't speak?

SARA looks up at him, blank. KORCZAK regards SARA for a moment.

Hmmmmm, I see, I see.

(to SARA) This is your violin?

STEFA: She won't let go of it.

KORCZAK: *(to STEFA)* Has she been playing it?

STEFA: No.

KORCZAK: *(to SARA)* Would you—would you play something for me? I hear you're very good at it.

> *Beat. SARA raises her bow.*

> *SARA plays him a piece that's technically difficult with many notes in it: La Folia (Variations 2 & 3) by Arcangelo Corelli.*

Sara, that's very . . . advanced—what a lot of notes.

> *SARA looks at him, nods slightly.*

Would you be able to play me something comforting? Something you'd play to a small child who's sick? Something you heard when you were a little girl?

> *SARA considers, then lifts her bow and plays a little tune, a Jewish lullaby: "Shlof Mayn Kind, Shlof Keseyder." After a minute she breaks off.*

(before she lowers her bow) It's beautiful. Will you keep playing?

> *SARA plays a few more notes. It goes scratchy. She looks at KORCZAK.*

Keep playing, if you can.

> *With difficulty SARA lifts her bow and keeps playing a few notes. Stops. She starts to cry, hunched over. A beat of her crying, breaking down.*

I'm sorry, I'm sorry: your mother, your father, I'm sorry, I'm sorry, it must hurt so much.

KORCZAK holds SARA.

(low) Stefa? A glass of milk?

STEFA: *(low)* Yes.

As STEFA turns to go, METTYE runs into the office.

METTYE: *(seeing SARA)* You're . . . here, you're . . . ! I didn't know where you were!

(to STEFA and KORCZAK) I didn't know where she was!

STEFA: Go out, Mettye, we're in the middle of an / examination—

METTYE runs over to SARA and throws her arms around her.

METTYE: *(to STEFA and KORCZAK)* I went into the infirmary and she wasn't there!

STEFA: No, Mettye, no, be / gentle with her—!

METTYE: *(to SARA)* And then I heard the violin and I came running up the stairs and she's here!

KORCZAK: *(to METTYE, soothing)* She's here. She's all right.

METTYE: *(to SARA)* You can play that violin! I didn't even know if you could play it! I thought maybe you just liked to hold a violin!!!

KORCZAK: Mettye, you found her, she's here: I'm going to take a few more minutes with her—

STEFA: Go out, go out, you . . .

STEFA sees her locket hanging around METTYE's neck.

That's my locket.

METTYE: What?

Beat.

STEFA: Go out, Mettye, right now!

METTYE: I found this in the infirmary—

STEFA: You stole it—

METTYE: No!

STEFA: Go out!

METTYE: No?! No, I found this locket—?!

STEFA: No you didn't—

METTYE: —in the infirmary—yes, I did. Under a cot.

STEFA: Mettye—

METTYE: It's true! I'm not lying! I'm not!!!!

SARA: *(low)* She's not lying.

Beat. They all turn and look at her.

(low) He came into the infirmary and he hid it, under a cot. I saw him do it.

> *She turns to* METTYE.

The boy. Israel.

> *Transition.*

Scene Nine.

KORCZAK and STEFA are in KORCZAK's office. KORCZAK is rubbing his eyes. He stops. Then he starts rubbing them again.

STEFA: Don't.

KORCZAK: What—what?

STEFA: *Don't. Rub. Them.*

KORCZAK: I can't give my eyes a little rub if I want to?

STEFA: They get red and they hurt you, and then you go up and down outside your office, "Oh Stefa, my eyes, ay, ay, ay—!"

KORCZAK: All right, all right, no rubbing, no rubbing my eyes: Germans in our country and no rubbing my eyes!

A tense beat of waiting. KORCZAK goes to rub his eyes again but then looks at STEFA and doesn't.

ISRAEL appears in the doorway.

ISRAEL: Doctor?

KORCZAK holds out the locket for him to see. ISRAEL eyes him, eyes the locket.

I'll come in, then?

> *ISRAEL comes and sits down in the chair in front of STEFA and KORCZAK. KORCZAK gets up and goes over to ISRAEL. ISRAEL flinches a little.*

KORCZAK: It's all right: I won't hit you.

> *Beat.*

It's hard and life hasn't offered you much. You should tell me why you took it.

ISRAEL: I didn't.

KORCZAK: You haven't lied to me since I met you.

ISRAEL: Yes I have.

STEFA: *(to ISRAEL)* What else have you stolen?

KORCZAK: Why? Why did you take it?

> *KORCZAK sighs.*

(to ISRAEL, low, sincere) Please. Make at least one . . . catastrophic attempt.

> *Beat. ISRAEL looks away.*

Look at me.

> *KORCZAK moves toward ISRAEL.*

> *ISRAEL flinches back, a reflex. KORCZAK gets hold of him.*

(frustrated) Look at me—I'm not—

Simultaneous text:

I'm not going to hit you.

ISRAEL: *(rushed)* She tore up my . . . !

KORCZAK: What? What did you say?

ISRAEL: *(low)* She tore up . . .

KORCZAK: She tore up . . . what?

ISRAEL: *(low)* It was just a drawing.

KORCZAK: She—who tore up your drawing?

Beat.

STEFA: I did.

KORCZAK turns toward STEFA.

KORCZAK: You—you did? Why? What was the drawing of?

STEFA: It wasn't a nice . . . he was doing it to . . . make trouble—it was an ugly drawing of . . .

KORCZAK: What was it?

STEFA: A man holding a bucket filled with blood.

ISRAEL goes to walk out. KORCZAK gets hold of him before he can go, and ISRAEL starts to struggle.

KORCZAK: No, no, look at me, what was the drawing of—?

ISRAEL: I was trying to . . . !

Beat.

I was trying to remember something.

KORCZAK: Was it something that happened? To you? To . . . ? Was it something you saw?

ISRAEL: He died, and . . .

ISRAEL shrugs.

He was sick.

KORCZAK: Who? Who?

ISRAEL: My . . . father.

KORCZAK: Your father? The drawing was your father dying?

KORCZAK turns to STEFA.

The drawing was his: it belonged to him, Stefa. It meant something to him.

STEFA: *(to KORCZAK)* I thought it was . . . I thought . . .

(to ISRAEL) I shouldn't have torn it up. I . . . I'm sorry.

Transition.

Intermezzo Six.

The PERFORMER PLAYING SARA speaks into a microphone. KORCZAK and METTYE are there.

PERFORMER PLAYING SARA: *(to audience)* The roof of the orphanage. The doctor and Mettye look down on the labyrinthine streets. Through the fog, they see the barbed wire and brick walls that divide the ghetto from the city. Mettye has a birdcage.

The PERFORMER PLAYING SARA looks to the violin.

There's a bird in it, chirping, like this:

A sound on the violin: the sound is the bird chirping. And inside the birdcage held by METTYE, there is a lit candle.

Transition.

Scene Ten.

KORCZAK: I had a bird when I was your age. A canary. But this bird is wild: it can't belong to you.

METTYE: Yes it can, if I just keep it in the cage . . . ?

KORCZAK: Open it.

METTYE is hesitating, her hand on the cage door.

METTYE: I don't want to.

KORCZAK: That was the contract.

Beat.

Go on.

METTYE vocalizes her reluctance as she opens the cage.

METTYE: Uhhhhh!

Beat. METTYE lifts the lit candle out of the cage and holds it in her hands (the bird has perched on her hands).

He's just sitting there. I don't think he wants to go.

KORCZAK: He's just been granted his freedom: he's deciding which way to fly.

METTYE: Oh.

KORCZAK: Things leave, Mettye. They leave us. It's not nice of them to go but it's sometimes in their nature. Like this bird. It's wild. It wants to fly off.

METTYE: But, look, it doesn't want to!

The bird flies away: a chirping sound on the violin indicates this. METTYE *blows out the candle.*

KORCZAK: There, it's gone.

METTYE: Oh. Oh, it's gone.

Beat.

It's gone.

KORCZAK: Yes.

They look off where the bird has gone.

Transition.

Scene Eleven.

We continue to hear the sound of a violin playing, far off. In a classroom, KORCZAK reads from a paper. ISRAEL, STEFA, and MISHA are present and waiting.

KORCZAK: *(mostly to ISRAEL)* This is the one hundred and eleventh session of the Children's Court. The session is closed because, Israel, you're a new ward, and it was felt this would be a better introduction to the court for you. A jury made up of five of your peers considered your case. They've asked that Misha, who witnessed what happened, tell you their verdict.

KORCZAK hands a piece of paper to MISHA.

MISHA: It says . . . "Israel, first, when the court was deliberating, we took into consideration how badly Mettye was beaten. We understand that Mettye's nose is still bleeding in the nights, and she's washing her sheets and blankets in the sinks. We ask that you go into the girl's dormitory, once a day, and wash her things for her." And they've written out the times of day when you can go in.

Beat.

"For the theft of Stefa's locket, the court took into consideration that Stefa destroyed property of Israel's—a drawing of his father—and that's why he took a locket containing a photograph of her mother.

We ask that in future Israel come to the Children's Court with any injustices committed against him by the staff, and we also ask him to apologize to Stefa in person within the week."

> *Beat.*

(to STEFA) "Stefa, the court's heard that you've already offered your regrets to Israel. We also ask that you offer us assurance that you won't destroy the property of a ward again. We would like this assurance in writing, and within the week."

> *KORCZAK looks at STEFA.*

> *STEFA nods.*

KORCZAK: Good, that ends the session.

> *STEFA, KORCZAK, and MISHA go out. On the way out, MISHA hands ISRAEL the Children's Court paper he's been reading. As they file out, METTYE comes in looking for ISRAEL.*

METTYE: You were . . . ? The court was in here?

> *ISRAEL nods.*

What . . . happened?

ISRAEL: Your bed has blood in it?

METTYE: Yeah!

> *Beat.*

ISRAEL: A lot of—?

METTYE: Yeah, a lot. Mmhmm. Yeah.

Beat.

ISRAEL: I'm . . . washing your . . . blankets, that's the . . . That's what the court . . .

METTYE: Yeah?

Beat.

The doctor and I were . . . Yesterday, I let my bird go and the doctor said . . . you . . . ? The doctor says you think . . . that I'm . . . ? He said . . . I think he was saying that you . . . like me, and if that's true, *don't break my nose*: try something else.

Beat.

ISRAEL: Like . . . what—?

METTYE: You like me? You do. That's . . . That's . . .

Beat.

ISRAEL: Yeah?

METTYE: Yeah. Maybe. Yeah.

Beat.

ISRAEL: Yeah?

SARA and MISHA come in. MISHA stops short at the door. He's hold-ing a bowl of food in his hands.

SARA: Mettye.

SARA goes to METTYE *right away, but* MISHA *stands there looking at* ISRAEL *and his proximity to* METTYE.

MISHA: What's he doing to you—should I call Stefa? She was just in here, / she's not far . . .

(out the door) Stefa! Stefa!

METTYE: No, it's fine: it's fine, he's not going to do anything.

MISHA: I'll get Stefa.

METTYE: No, it's fine—

But ISRAEL *walks quickly toward* MISHA.

(to ISRAEL*)* No!

When ISRAEL *gets to* MISHA, *he knocks his bowl of food out of his hands. It spills all over the floor.*

Time suspends. There is a drone on the violin. The young perform-ers are at microphones.

PERFORMER PLAYING METTYE: *(to audience)* Misha's soup spills on the floor. It's ruined. Misha picks the bowl up and throws it at Israel. Israel knocks him down.

Beat.

(to audience) When Israel steps on Misha's legs, this is the sound Misha's bones make:

The PERFORMER PLAYING METTYE breaks a piece of chalk into the microphone, to make the sound effect.

(to audience) And the thought Israel has is:

PERFORMER PLAYING ISRAEL: *(to audience)* Like chalk.

We go back into real time. MISHA lies on the ground. ISRAEL stands over him. The sound cuts back in. METTYE is screaming. STEFA comes running into the room.

STEFA: Mettye! Mettye! What!? Have you been murdered? Stop screaming like that!

KORCZAK follows STEFA into the room and takes in the scene. METTYE is still screaming. MISHA on the ground. ISRAEL backs up, turns, and runs out.

KORCZAK: *(to ISRAEL)* Wait—wait! Where are you . . . going?

KORCZAK turns back to MISHA.

The lights start to fade.

Misha, why're you . . . ? Misha!

Lights fade to black.

End of Act One.

Intermission.

Act Two

Prologue.

The PERFORMERS PLAYING METTYE, ISRAEL, MISHA, and SARA come on stage while the house lights are up. They rub chalk on their hands and make chalk prints of their hands on the walls.

Violin music.

The PERFORMER PLAYING ISRAEL goes off stage. The PERFORMERS PLAYING METTYE and MISHA cross out the date "1940" on the stage and write in chalk beside it:

1942.

And they cross out the number 400,000 (Jews sealed in with a brick wall and barbed wire). They change the number to:

317,000

They turn out to the audience.

They regard them in the gloom.

Transition.

Scene One.

We're in KORCZAK's office. KORCZAK is writing. STEFA stands in front of him and refers to a notebook. We hear SARA practising violin, off.

KORCZAK: *(without looking up)* Where to?

STEFA: The Bermans. He's going to give us twenty kilos of bread. And blankets he said he'd be willing to donate—

KORCZAK: You go to the Bermans.

STEFA: No.

KORCZAK looks up.

He likes you.

KORCZAK: The last time I was over there he just stood and stared at me with his mouth hanging open, so either he doesn't like me or it's sclerosis of the brain.

Beat.

(to explain) Sclerosis—hardening—his brain has hardened.

STEFA: He's in awe.

KORCZAK: Of what?

STEFA: Your fame.

KORCZAK: Fame—*what fame?*

STEFA: Janusz.

KORCZAK: What?

STEFA: Go to the Bermans. And put your—wear your arm band.

KORCZAK: Why? I know I'm Jewish!

STEFA: Janusz. Wear your goddamn arm band.

KORCZAK: Fine, fine.

> *KORCZAK rubs his eyes, pushes his writing away, and gets up and puts on his jacket and his arm band.*

I saw forty-four of the children.

STEFA: And?

KORCZAK: No typhus. No lice. The worst thing is they've become fascinated by their own diseases. They're like old people.

> *Beat.*

I told the new one, with the fever—Henryk—that if he didn't drink his cup of tea it would become very sad and it would go and throw itself under a streetcar. He drank the tea.

> *Beat.*

There are three more children in the infirmary with stomach complaints. I think it's the bread from the Supply Section, I think they mixed it with something. Sawdust? Cement? It tasted a little architectural.

Beat.

The flies in the toilet are taking over—it's a black swarm—they're building a whole civilization on the ceiling, with houses and streets. I wrote a note and stuck it to the back of the door: "While you're sitting here, kill some flies."

KORCZAK is standing in the doorway with his coat on now, about to leave. STEFA hesitates, about to speak.

What?

STEFA: I . . .

Beat.

KORCZAK: Spit it out—

STEFA: I went to the Kosskas. They had a telegram for us. The Tarnowskis—they can get the papers for her.

Beat.

They have the papers for Sara—

KORCZAK: I heard you: they've paid off a guard?

STEFA nods.

Polish?

STEFA: German.

KORCZAK: And she'll be?

STEFA: A cousin.

Beat.

KORCZAK: We take her to the gate—

STEFA: We take her to the iron gate—the German guard is there—the Tarnowskis wait for her on the Aryan side.

KORCZAK: And then?

STEFA: She's their cousin.

KORCZAK: So she's . . . ?

STEFA: She's visiting.

KORCZAK: She's visiting a bombed-out city? She's—why? Why would she visit a bombed-out city? And if they ask for her papers, on the streetcar, she'll have to say to them, "Yes, my name is . . . *(gestures)* . . . "

STEFA: Tarnowski.

KORCZAK: And you think, when she's frightened, she'll be able to remember all that?

STEFA: Yes.

Beat.

KORCZAK: She lost her mother and father: she'll lose you; she'll lose Mettye—

STEFA: She'll have the Tarnowskis.

KORCZAK: Who the hell are they!

STEFA: She'll be fine.

Beat. A standoff.

The sound of pounding at the courtyard door, off, down the corridor.

It distracts them both for a moment.

KORCZAK: *(to STEFA)* You don't know if she'll be fine. She *might* be fine—

STEFA: They offered you papers as well, and a passage out of the ghetto.

More pounding at the door, off, down the corridor, the courtyard door. KORCZAK looks toward the sound.

KORCZAK: *(calling to MISHA)* Misha!

(calling, frustrated) Misha? Go to the door! Tell them to wait.

Beat.

Misha!

STEFA: Yes?

KORCZAK: Yes what!

STEFA: About Sara.

More pounding on the door.

KORCZAK: *(to STEFA)* She'd have to walk to the—you'd have to get her to agree to walk to the gate—Misha!

MISHA: *(calling from off)* I am!

STEFA: *(referring to SARA)* So yes?

Pause. They both listen to SARA playing the violin off in the house for a moment.

KORCZAK: *(of the violin tune)* This is a pretty one.

Pause. Violin.

STEFA: Yes?

MISHA runs in and stands there, shocked.

(to MISHA) What?

Beat.

What?

MISHA: He's back.

STEFA: Who?

ISRAEL walks in behind MISHA. His clothes are dirty and ragged. ISRAEL's pale. He has a bloody rag tied on his arm, and his shirt sleeve is soaked in blood.

ISRAEL: Doctor?

Beat.

KORCZAK: You—you . . . you're . . . back—you're back. Where have you
. . . been?

ISRAEL stumbles.

You're hurt?

ISRAEL: Yeah.

KORCZAK: *(to STEFA)* Will you get the . . .

STEFA nods.

STEFA: Yes.

(to MISHA) Misha.

STEFA goes out, pulling MISHA out with her.

KORCZAK: It—it's your arm? Anywhere else?

ISRAEL: No.

KORCZAK examines ISRAEL's arm.

KORCZAK: You were in a fight?

ISRAEL: Uh, not—no.

KORCZAK: How?

ISRAEL: He . . . had a . . .

KORCZAK: A knife?

ISRAEL: It was—no. A . . . broken . . . it was a . . . *(gestures, feeble)* . . . bottle I think.

KORCZAK: When?

ISRAEL: Uh.

KORCZAK: Two days ago? Three.

ISRAEL: Yeah.

> *KORCZAK touches the arm near the wound. ISRAEL grimaces.*

KORCZAK: This hurts?

ISRAEL: Yeah.

KORCZAK: I need to know if you're fevered.

> *ISRAEL nods.*

> *KORCZAK puts a hand on ISRAEL's forehead, then one to his own forehead.*

> *STEFA re-enters with iodine, bandages.*

> *KORCZAK takes the medical supplies and opens the bottle of iodine.*

(to ISRAEL) This'll hurt.

> *ISRAEL nods.*

KORCZAK disinfects the wound.

ISRAEL breathes out through his teeth.

KORCZAK starts tweezing and bandaging ISRAEL's arm, picking glass out of his wound and dropping it in a basin.

Where have you been?

ISRAEL shrugs.

Where did you go? Back to Gesia Street? I went there—I looked for you.

ISRAEL: Yeah?

KORCZAK: Where were you? You . . . were there?

ISRAEL: Yeah.

KORCZAK: That street . . . It burned to the ground. Then I went to the morgue—I thought . . . I looked for you, for months. Are you eating?

ISRAEL: Yeah.

KORCZAK: How?

ISRAEL: My arm's bad?

KORCZAK: It's—yes.

ISRAEL: How bad?

KORCZAK: This is why you came here?

ISRAEL: Yeah?

KORCZAK: Where are you living? You're in the street?

(to STEFA) Will you make up a bed for him?

> *STEFA doesn't move.*

Stefa?

> *STEFA stands there. In response, ISRAEL tries to stand up.*

(to ISRAEL) No, sit down—

(to STEFA) Stefa—

STEFA: For how long?

ISRAEL: *(of his injury)* Is it fixed?

KORCZAK: It's—no. Your arm's infected.

STEFA: *(to KORCZAK)* A week?

ISRAEL: *(to STEFA)* I'll go.

> *ISRAEL tries to stand again. KORCZAK, panicked, goes to stop him physically.*

KORCZAK: *(to ISRAEL)* No, you won't. No!

> *KORCZAK turns back to STEFA.*

Stefa.

STEFA: *(to KORCZAK)* How long?

KORCZAK: He's come back. He's one of our wards.

>   *Beat.*

Stefa, please—

STEFA: And Sara?

KORCZAK: I'll—yes.

>   *Beat.*

Yes, all right. I'll talk to her.

>   *STEFA turns to ISRAEL.*

STEFA: *(to ISRAEL)* No one goes out. The street entrance is bricked up. We use the courtyard door for deliveries.

ISRAEL: I saw.

STEFA: No one goes out.

>   *Beat.*

Yes?

KORCZAK: *(to STEFA)* It's all right. Make up the bed.

>   *Transition.*

Scene Two.

A day later, in a classroom. MISHA, SARA, *and* METTYE *are there.* SARA *is tuning her violin,* METTYE *is restless, unable to focus on the blackboard and studying she's doing, and* MISHA *is reading from a little black book.*

METTYE: *(to MISHA)* Did you see his arm?

MISHA: It looked bad.

METTYE: It did?

MISHA: Yeah, it was black.

METTYE: Black.

MISHA: Black, yeah, and bleeding. They'll probably cut it off.

METTYE: They will?!

MISHA: I'm—no—how would I know?

METTYE pushes his head, frustrated with being teased.

METTYE: Did he look the same?

MISHA: He—no—his face was . . . I thought he might have typhus.

METTYE: He was . . . fevered-looking? Was he pale?

MISHA: He's just down the corridor, Mettye. You're going to see him soon: then you can look at him all you want and ask him all your questions.

METTYE: Did you say anything to him about your legs?

MISHA: Like what?

> *METTYE trails off because ISRAEL's standing in the doorway. His arm is bandaged.*

> *He's still pale, unwell.*

> *SARA breaks off playing.*

> *METTYE, SARA, and MISHA all stand up and look at ISRAEL.*

> *Pause.*

METTYE: You're back.

> *Beat.*

You should be in the infirmary.

ISRAEL: Yeah.

> *Beat.*

METTYE: Where were you, all this time?

ISRAEL: The ghetto.

METTYE: Misha was in the infirmary, for seven months, in a cot. You broke both his legs.

ISRAEL: *(to MISHA)* Are they . . . better?

MISHA: Yeah.

METTYE: Why did you leave like that?

    ISRAEL shrugs.

What does that mean? What does the shrug mean?

ISRAEL: It means . . . I don't remember.

METTYE: What's it like out there now, in the ghetto? Did you see people with typhus?

    ISRAEL shrugs and nods.

Is it—are they out on the street? Lying on the street?

ISRAEL: Yeah.

METTYE: Are they dead?

ISRAEL: Some of them.

METTYE: What's it like . . . out there?

ISRAEL: Crowded.

METTYE: *(touching his arm)* You were . . . cut, or . . . ?

ISRAEL nods.

Someone did that?

ISRAEL: Yeah.

METTYE: Who?

ISRAEL shrugs.

And, what? You . . .

ISRAEL: I wrapped a cloth around it, and . . .

METTYE: And what?

ISRAEL: It didn't work, and it . . . got worse, and I . . . came here. I . . . don't feel . . .

ISRAEL holds a chair, unsteady on his feet.

METTYE: Are you . . . ? Are you all right?

(to MISHA) Is he all right—is he going to faint?

MISHA: *(to ISRAEL)* You should go back to the infirmary.

ISRAEL nods at MISHA.

ISRAEL: *(to METTYE)* I'll go then.

ISRAEL goes out. METTYE walks to look down the corridor.

METTYE: *(to MISHA)* Is he going to faint, in the corridor?

MISHA: I don't know.

METTYE: Should we get help, or . . . ?

MISHA: If he faints, in the corridor, then yes, we should get help.

METTYE: Why did he do that: go out of the infirmary and come down here?

SARA: To talk to you.

METTYE: But why? He just . . . wanted to see all of us again, see if we're the same?

SARA: No, he wanted to see you.

METTYE realizes what she means. Blushes.

METTYE: No he didn't.

But SARA has started to pluck the "Wedding March" on her violin.

Don't! That's not funny, don't! Stop! He'll hear.

SARA plays the "Wedding March."

Sara!

Transition.

Intermezzo One.

The PERFORMER PLAYING MISHA turns to the audience and speaks into a microphone. KORCZAK comes on stage. He sits and writes.

PERFORMER PLAYING MISHA: *(to audience)* Korczak's office. Mid-afternoon. The doctor's jotting down notes to himself in his journal. His hands are chapped from the cold.

> *On cue, KORCZAK drops his pen. He stretches his fingers out and blows on them. He goes over to a chair and balances it on two of its legs.*

This morning, in the ghetto, he saw a girl, four years old, lying in a doorway, heaving. He knelt down and talked to her until she died. When he got back, he started writing down some notes to himself on advanced starvation and what it looks like in children, to keep himself from . . .

> *KORCZAK knocks the chair over, watches it fall.*

> *He goes back to his desk and keeps writing.*

As he writes, he hears the firm footsteps of Stefa coming down the corridor toward him . . .

KORCZAK—and through him the audience—pauses and listens to the footsteps coming toward him.

. . . and he picks up the pace.

KORCZAK scribbles hard for a moment, swiftly turning pages.

Transition.

Scene Three.

STEFA enters and immediately starts reading from a list.

STEFA: You're writing.

KORCZAK: Mm. As you can see.

STEFA: Finish that up.

KORCZAK: I'm—look! Look how fast I'm writing, Stefa! My hand is flying across the page—there!

KORCZAK closes his notebook.

STEFA: Try Marek Stein, Yosef Kanal, and the Czerniakows. Try to get them to give you food, not money. We need bread, we're . . . We need bread. Then go to the council, to Altman, he should have a shipment for you—

KORCZAK: "It's our children," he says, then he offers me a cigarette from a gold case: "It's our children."

STEFA: Janusz.

KORCZAK: What? It's my fault the man's a—

STEFA: Janusz.

KORCZAK: An "F major"?

ISRAEL is in the doorway, listening in on STEFA and KORCZAK.

How low are we?

STEFA: Get him to give you bread.

ISRAEL: You told me to come . . . ?

KORCZAK: *(to STEFA)* Israel knows the streets. I need the help, Stefa.

Beat.

STEFA: *(to KORCZAK)* Curfew is at eight.

STEFA goes out.

KORCZAK: I have to go to Dzielna Street: there's an orphanage there. I said I would look in on it. I was thinking Zelasna?

Beat.

No?

ISRAEL: They shoot down onto it.

KORCZAK: Which one, then?

ISRAEL: Take Twarda.

KORCZAK: Why?

ISRAEL: It's narrow—it's factories—you won't see the . . . *(gestures)* . . .

KORCZAK: The . . . what? The worst?

ISRAEL: That place, on Dzielna, the windows are burned out and there's no food.

KORCZAK: You've been there?

ISRAEL shrugs.

ISRAEL: Yeah?

KORCZAK: Is that . . . how you've been getting food? At orphanages . . . ? Or . . . soup kitchens? Or in the streets, you asked for ten groszy? Or you stole it? From the dead. From the dying?

Beat.

It's all right, it's good you got it somehow.

ISRAEL: You don't let anyone go out?

KORCZAK: No: typhus.

ISRAEL: Typhus is not that bad.

KORCZAK: Right now, but there'll be another outbreak. And the children are—some of them are weak—it would be easy for them to catch it. That and I . . . don't want them to see what's happening in the ghetto.

ISRAEL: Yeah?

KORCZAK: I want there to be some children left who haven't been changed by the war, who don't think it's normal for people to be shot in the street.

Beat.

You've been in the streets—you've been living somehow—you've seen the worst: has there been anyone who's been . . . kind to you?

Beat.

ISRAEL: Like who?

Beat.

KORCZAK: Tell me: do you . . . still think of your father? Do you remember him?

ISRAEL shrugs.

(pointing to ISRAEL's arm) The swelling's gone down.

ISRAEL: Yeah?

KORCZAK: Are you going to . . . stay?

Beat.

ISRAEL shrugs.

ISRAEL: *(very low)* Yeah.

KORCZAK smiles.

KORCZAK: Yes? Good. That's good.

Beat.

Why do you . . . want to stay here, at the orphanage?

ISRAEL shrugs.

ISRAEL: The last place was . . .

ISRAEL shrugs.

Beat.

Here it's . . . dry.

KORCZAK: *(low)* I think of you as *my child*, you know that, don't you?

Beat. ISRAEL looks at him, wary, interested.

ISRAEL: Yeah?

KORCZAK reaches out and touches his face.

KORCZAK: *(low)* Israel.

ISRAEL: I'll . . . I'll go then?

Transition.

Intermezzo Two.

The PERFORMER PLAYING METTYE approaches the microphone.

PERFORMER PLAYING METTYE: *(to audience)* Evening. A corridor in the orphanage. The doctor listens for the faint sound of the violin . . .

KORCZAK listens.

We hear the sound of SARA playing the violin, faintly, off.

He lingers in the corridor, hesitating, listening . . .

KORCZAK listens, smiling, sad.

And then goes toward the sound.

Transition.

Scene Four.

SARA plays a little tune on the violin: it's the tune to the bird song that METTYE sings in Act One.

KORCZAK: That's a new one.

SARA looks up, sees KORCZAK standing there.

SARA: It's pretty, isn't it?

KORCZAK: Sara: I know this is your practice time, but . . . And I know Stefa's already spoken to you about the papers she's been trying to get for you.

Beat.

Well now she's got them.

Beat.

Do you remember Mr. Tarnowski? I know he liked your . . . violin playing . . . Before the war he met you, and your father, when your father played for the symphony . . . ?

SARA plays a few very ugly off-chord notes. Then to explain herself:

SARA: It's the A string. It's pulled a little tight.

SARA lifts her bow again.

KORCZAK: Sara—

SARA ignores him and plays the tune again, louder now, wilder.

Sara! / Sara, are you . . . !

SARA keeps playing, drowning KORCZAK out until he puts his hands on her violin strings to stop her playing.

They regard each other.

You're not talking?

SARA: I'm talking.

KORCZAK: Mr. Tarnowski has papers for you.

SARA: They'd say I'm Polish?

KORCZAK: And you'd—

SARA: I'd leave the ghetto.

KORCZAK: And you'd be Halinka Tarnowski.

SARA lifts her bow and makes a horrible screeching sound on the violin.

You don't like the name?

SARA raises her bow again but KORCZAK stops her.

No, listen: these papers will allow you to honour your father by playing the violin as he taught you to. They'll allow you to use your extraordinary talent: go out into the world and perform for many people and bring light into their lives, and that's what Stefa and I want for you. And so does Mettye, in her heart.

Beat.

You're meant to play for the whole world.

SARA looks at him and considers.

METTYE comes running into the room.

METTYE: *(to SARA)* You're playing it! I just heard you playing it!

(turning to KORCZAK) It's pretty, isn't it? Did she tell you I taught it to her?

Beat.

(looking between KORCZAK and SARA) What?

SARA: Nothing.

METTYE realizes.

It's—no, it's / nothing.

METTYE: *(clutching at SARA)* Oh no oh no oh no!

SARA: *(to METTYE)* I'm not going! It's fine, Mettye, it's fine. I'm not going.

Transition.

Scene Five.

ISRAEL stands outside a doorway, looking in. After a moment he backs up and METTYE comes skipping out. A beat as she looks at ISRAEL standing there.

METTYE: Are you going in to see the doctor?

ISRAEL: No, I was . . . No.

METTYE: He's in there.

ISRAEL: I wasn't—I was . . .

Beat.

I was waiting for you.

METTYE: Oh.

Beat.

How's your arm?

ISRAEL shrugs, shows it to her.

Beat.

Why are you . . . looking at me like that . . . ?

 ISRAEL looks away.

ISRAEL: You look . . .

METTYE: What?

ISRAEL: You look—you all look . . . like you have less . . . to eat.

 Beat.

METTYE: Yeah.

 Beat.

(touching them) My ribs.

 Beat.

You were waiting for me?

ISRAEL: Yeah.

METTYE: Why?

 ISRAEL shrugs.

 Beat.

ISRAEL: I brought you something.

 ISRAEL hands it to her. METTYE stares at it.

METTYE: What is it?

ISRAEL: Chocolate.

Beat.

METTYE: How did you . . . get it?! How did you . . . ? Did you *sell your soul?*

Beat.

How would you get this . . . ?

ISRAEL shrugs.

ISRAEL walks away.

Wait. You—thank you!

He's gone.

METTYE looks down at the chocolate.

(to no one) Chocolate.

Transition.

Intermezzo Three.

The PERFORMER PLAYING METTYE approaches and turns to the audience. She speaks into a microphone.

PERFORMER PLAYING METTYE: *(to audience)* The doctor's in his office: with Stefa.

STEFA comes on holding a knife. She hands it to KORCZAK.

This morning Stefa stripped down the beds, and under one of them, secured to the underside of it with string, she found a bag filled with . . .

KORCZAK holds the knife up and looks at it. It gleams in the light.

. . . food rations, money, chocolate bars, and a knife.

STEFA and KORCZAK look at each other.

Transition.

Scene Six.

KORCZAK is pacing—restless, waiting.

STEFA is standing stock-still.

ISRAEL arrives in the doorway.

ISRAEL: I'll come in, then and . . .

ISRAEL trails off because he's seen what KORCZAK's holding.

That's mine.

KORCZAK: Yes, I know: Stefa found it.

Beat.

You—when? When did you go out and get it? It was hidden somewhere in the ghetto?

Beat.

Last night?

Beat.

Two days ago?

    Beat.

STEFA: *(to KORCZAK)* There's an outbreak of typhus at the hospital.

ISRAEL: I didn't go there.

STEFA: *(to KORCZAK)* And if he went to the graveyard—

KORCZAK: *(to ISRAEL)* No? Then where did you go? And how did you get all this? You're stealing, you're smuggling?

ISRAEL: Yeah.

KORCZAK: Which one?

    ISRAEL shrugs.

ISRAEL: Both.

KORCZAK: You're smuggling. You go out of the ghetto?

ISRAEL: Yeah.

KORCZAK: The patrols, they don't—do they see you?

    ISRAEL shrugs.

No?

ISRAEL: Yeah, sometimes.

KORCZAK: They shoot at you?

ISRAEL shrugs.

ISRAEL: Yeah?

KORCZAK: You could be caught and hanged.

ISRAEL shrugs.

ISRAEL: Yeah.

Beat.

Most people are . . .

KORCZAK: Are what?

ISRAEL: Dying.

KORCZAK: Your arm—is that how it got cut?

ISRAEL: A Pole saw me, on the Aryan side, and . . . threw a bottle at me.

KORCZAK: *(re: the knife)* Did you steal this? From a German?

Beat.

What were you going to do with it?

ISRAEL: Use it.

KORCZAK: For what?

ISRAEL: Or sell it.

KORCZAK: To who?

> *Pause.* KORCZAK *offers* ISRAEL *his knife back.* ISRAEL *looks at it but doesn't take it.*

If you stay here, you'll keep smuggling?

> *Beat.*

ISRAEL: I'll stop.

STEFA: He's lying.

> *Beat.*

KORCZAK: *(to* ISRAEL, *clinical)* If you're caught smuggling, you'll . . . This orphanage could be . . . closed, and these children, and there are two hundred of them, they might . . . be on the street, starving, and I would use all my ties, in the councils, but I might not be able to . . . stop that. Do you . . . can you . . . comprehend what it would mean for these children to . . . die, and for it to be . . . because of something you did?

> *Beat.*

(clinical) Do you . . . have anything—anything left in you that I can trust?

> *Beat.*

ISRAEL: You want me to not lie?

> *Beat.*

KORCZAK: Yes.

ISRAEL: You're doing well, in here, but it's getting worse, and . . . you're probably going to run out of food.

Beat.

ISRAEL shrugs.

ISRAEL: Then . . . what different does it make what I do?

Transition.

Scene Seven.

We're in KORCZAK's office.

KORCZAK examines a rash on MISHA's arm: MISHA's sleeve is rolled up. MISHA holds a small black book in his hands.

KORCZAK: This hurts . . . ?

MISHA shrugs.

Stings . . . ?

MISHA shrugs, nods.

How long has it been there?

MISHA: Two weeks.

KORCZAK: *(a statement)* You're favouring this leg.

MISHA shrugs.

This one still hurts you?

MISHA: Sometimes. I've lost more weight?

KORCZAK: You haven't lost any height. There's some good news.

KORCZAK sits down beside him.

What are you reading?

MISHA hands it to him. KORCZAK looks at it, leafs through it.

The Torah.

MISHA: Yes.

KORCZAK: Is it any good?

MISHA: It's—yeah: parts of it.

KORCZAK hands the black book back to MISHA.

KORCZAK: Read me a passage. Go on. Read me something. Something cheerful. Something about how God feels about Germans.

MISHA: Where's that?

KORCZAK: I don't know.

Beat.

You're thinking something over, Misha? What is it?

MISHA: He had food rations?

KORCZAK: He did, yes.

MISHA: From . . . smuggling?

KORCZAK: Is that what you're thinking about? Food?

MISHA: We—we're . . . low on food.

KORCZAK: We . . .

Beat.

MISHA: We are?

There's a commotion in the building, off stage.

KORCZAK: We—yes.

KORCZAK and MISHA listen for a moment to the commotion, distracted.

MISHA: What's happening?

KORCZAK listens.

KORCZAK: I don't know: stay here for a minute—

METTYE, STEFA, and SARA burst in. METTYE's forehead has been cut and blood is dripping down her face.

What happened?

STEFA: They knocked her down. Her forehead's cut—there's blood in her mouth—

KORCZAK: Mettye. Look at me.

STEFA: *(to KORCZAK)* Is it her eye . . . ?

KORCZAK: Her eye's all right: the cut's deep.

ISRAEL enters and stands in the doorway.

Who was it?

STEFA: ss. They were asking for all of us to come out into the street. I told them they had the wrong address and to go and speak to Altman and the council, and then Mettye came running up to the doorway and they knocked her down—

METTYE: *(to KORCZAK)* It's bad?

KORCZAK: *(to METTYE)* It's a bad cut, but that's all it is.

STEFA: *(to KORCZAK)* Then they left. There were a lot of people, running, in the streets. I don't know why—

METTYE: My mouth hurts.

SARA: Mettye—

KORCZAK: She's all right, Sara, get out of the way.

KORCZAK picks up METTYE and carries her out, STEFA and SARA following. ISRAEL and MISHA are alone. They look at each other.

MISHA: They—they knocked her down: she's cut and . . . bleeding.

ISRAEL: Yeah, I saw.

Beat.

MISHA: We're low on . . . food, in here. That's what the doctor just said.

ISRAEL: Yeah?

MISHA: Do you think . . . we'll get lower?

Beat.

ISRAEL: Yeah.

MISHA: Yeah.

Beat.

I ate the straw out of my mattress one time, when I still lived with my grandmother. I think it was rotting—it cut my mouth. I remember what it was like to be . . . hungry like that.

Beat.

I couldn't . . . get up.

Beat.

We're going to be . . . lying on our beds, not moving much, and then . . . some of us will be alive and some dead, and the doctor will be . . . watching that, and . . .

Beat.

What about you? What are you going to do?

Transition.

Intermezzo Four.

The PERFORMER PLAYING SARA *speaks into the microphone.*

PERFORMER PLAYING SARA: *(to audience)* The doctor's in his office, look-ing through old notes.

On cue, KORCZAK *looks through old notes.*

The crumbling walls of the orphanage irritate his lungs and make him cough.

KORCZAK coughs, then wipes his mouth with a pocket handkerchief.

Outside, searchlights. Dogs. Gunfire.

A spotlight, operated by the PERFORMER PLAYING METTYE, *moves quickly across the stage.*

He finds what he's looking for.

KORCZAK finds a slim manuscript.

Something he wrote a year or so ago: an allegory about the sun.

Transition.

Scene Eight.

KORCZAK is in his office, sitting at his desk, reading over a slim manuscript. STEFA enters and is holding a bottle of vodka.

STEFA: Janusz?

KORCZAK looks up.

How's Mettye.

KORCZAK: She broke a tooth when she fell—she's sitting up and looking at herself in the mirror: she's vain about the tooth.

Beat. STEFA puts the bottle of vodka on his desk.

STEFA: I went to Altman. He had this: a bottle of vodka. The Gestapo are shutting it all down, the Supply Section is closed, the Transfer Station is closed. There's nothing getting through. There's nothing in the ghetto. None of them had anything for us. He said in a week or two.

KORCZAK: A week or two?

Pause.

STEFA: We . . . We can't . . . wait a week or two, and . . . nothing's getting through.

Pause.

KORCZAK rubs his eyes.

Israel and Misha aren't back?

KORCZAK shakes his head.

KORCZAK: No.

Beat.

The Germans are going to evacuate the hospital. They're being sent to work in the East. The sick and dying are going to work in the East. What will they do—build themselves a hospital? The world is going mad.

Last week I said to Altman, "There are children dying in the streets, I want a shelter for them." One of the empty storefronts and some fuel, wood or coal, and a few attendants to help get them there. Most of them are at such an advanced stage of starvation that they can't get up. I won't try to help them to live; I won't feed them; I'm not asking for medicine; I'll just give them a place to die. With someone stroking their hair. And he said, "Do you want bread for your children or do you want the shelter?"

KORCZAK rubs his eyes.

STEFA: Don't rub them.

KORCZAK: I . . . write notes to myself, in my journal, on the rights of children to a moral education. I'm going to watch as we run out of food. I should take notes: "the effect of *starvation* on the morality of children."

Beat.

The Germans are in the streets and Mettye's lost a tooth and where are Israel and Misha? Stefa . . . Stefa . . . I . . .

KORCZAK cries. STEFA holds KORCZAK.

STEFA: Sh. Sh.

Beat. STEFA holds him.

Sh. Sh. Sh.

KORCZAK rubs his eyes.

Don't. Rub. Them.

Beat.

Tomorrow, you'll go back out, find a policeman to help you in the streets, go to the Kosskas and the Bermans, go back to the council.

KORCZAK nods.

KORCZAK: Yes.

Beat.

STEFA: Janusz?

STEFA puts papers down on his desk.

These are papers.

KORCZAK: Yes, I'll—I'll—yes, I'll talk to Sara again—

STEFA: They're not for Sara. They're for you.

KORCZAK: No.

Beat.

No! Don't be stupid, I'm not going to argue with you. I've said to you, I've said to Altman, I said to that German who knew me: I'm not going to leave the children. I'm not going to go out of the ghetto without them: they're *my children*—

STEFA: I'd stay with them—

KORCZAK: No.

STEFA: You'd go, to the West. You'd publish, you're a doctor, you'd—

KORCZAK: No, and what? And there would be two hundred starving children in here with you? No. No. You want me to talk to Sara again, I will.

STEFA: Yes, do that.

KORCZAK: Fine.

Beat.

STEFA: Fine.

Beat.

(off KORCZAK's *look)* No matter what . . . happens, at least we'll be here with them. To . . . see them through and . . . yes.

STEFA *pours herself a glass of vodka.*

Transition.

Intermezzo Five.

The PERFORMER PLAYING METTYE approaches the audience.

PERFORMER PLAYING METTYE: *(to audience)* Stefa and the doctor have been running the orphanage together for thirty-one years.

KORCZAK holds her. They look at each other: knowing each other. Comforting each other.

A long time.

Transition.

Scene Nine.

KORCZAK hurries into the front corridor, passing STEFA, and hangs up his coat. There are a number of large sacks lying on the floor.

KORCZAK: The ghetto's empty—no one's in the streets—no one except the ss—no one's answering their doors—

STEFA: Janusz—

KORCZAK: There are blockades down on Leszno: I don't know which streets to take—

STEFA: Janusz, Janusz—

KORCZAK: What—what! I'm not deaf!

STEFA points to the large sacks of bread sitting in a doorway.

What?

STEFA: It's bread.

(calling) MISHA!

Pause. KORCZAK looks at the sacks of bread.

MISHA! MISHA!

KORCZAK: It's . . .

Beat.

STEFA: MISHA!

KORCZAK: *(to STEFA)* They're . . . back?

MISHA and then ISRAEL come in.

STEFA: *(to MISHA)* Come in. Tell the doctor.

Beat.

Tell him.

Beat.

MISHA: It's . . . bread.

Beat.

We got it.

Beat.

We went out, to the Aryan side, we got—it was—we got . . . knives, some German knives. We went to get . . . pistols, but the Poles on the other side didn't have any for us, and . . . we came back with the—we got through, there's a hole in one of the factory walls—and we gave them the knives and they gave us the bread. They brought it here for us in a wagon. They want to fight the Germans: they have knives, and pistols and gun powder . . .

MISHA trails off.

(to KORCZAK) Doctor? Are you . . . ?

(to STEFA) What's wrong with him?

STEFA: He's fine.

KORCZAK: *(to MISHA and ISRAEL)* You . . . got us bread?

MISHA: Yes! We did it. We got bread. A lot of it.

KORCZAK gets up and goes to MISHA, holds him. Breaks down.

KORCZAK: You got us . . . ? You got us . . . ? Israel, you . . .

MISHA: Stefa, what's wrong with him?

STEFA: He's fine.

Transition.

Scene Ten.

We're in a hallway in the orphanage at night, outside of the girls' dormitory, where METTYE *is waiting.*

METTYE: *(whispering call)* Israel! Israel.

ISRAEL turns and sees her, comes over to her.

I've been . . . waiting for you.

ISRAEL points to METTYE's forehead.

ISRAEL: Does it hurt?

METTYE: Oh, that. There are stitches. Do you see them? They're in my hair. Black stitches like on a shirt.

ISRAEL: Can I see your tooth?

METTYE: It's in the street.

ISRAEL: Let's see the gap.

METTYE: *(covering her mouth)* No! Why? It's a gap. It's fine, I'll just be ugly, with a *gap in my teeth*.

Beat.

ISRAEL: You were . . . waiting for me?

METTYE: Yes—mmmhmm—yes, I . . .

Beat. METTYE is distracted. ISRAEL is moving closer to her.

You . . . ? You left—you've been going out of the ghetto? And you . . . got all that bread?

Beat. He nods.

Is it . . . ? What's it like . . . out there?

Beat.

ISRAEL shrugs.

ISRAEL: Some of the buildings are gone, but more trees, there's trees and uh . . . birds. And . . . food. And people are . . . *(gestures)* . . . it's like how you remember it.

METTYE: Were you scared?

ISRAEL shrugs.

You shrug a lot.

ISRAEL shrugs.

Well don't shrug again. Say something.

ISRAEL: Like what?

METTYE: Like . . . the thoughts you're having in your head.

Pause.

ISRAEL: You're . . . pretty.

Beat.

METTYE doesn't know what she's saying.

METTYE: I—I was . . . I . . . I don't remember what I was . . . saying . . . and—

ISRAEL kisses METTYE. They're both nervous, unskilled. We see five beats of this. Then, a violin begins to play romantically, off: Nocturne op. 9, no. 2 in E-flat Major by Chopin.

METTYE turns and goes off stage.

(as she exits) SARA!

ISRAEL waits there, in the hallway, unsure what to do. STEFA enters and stands behind ISRAEL and listens to the following offstage conversation.

(off) SARA!!!! Stop!

The violin music breaks off abruptly.

SARA: (off) Oh, Israel.

METTYE: (off) Don't.

SARA: (off) "He's so good looking. Don't you think, Sara? Don't you think he's so good looking—?"

METTYE: *(off)* Give me that.

> *METTYE re-enters. She sees STEFA.*

Oh. Stefa.

> *ISRAEL turns around and sees STEFA.*

I'm sorry, we didn't mean to wake you, or . . . I'm sorry.

STEFA: Mettye.

> *STEFA passes METTYE, touching her face as she goes by. She stops at ISRAEL.*

Israel.

> *ISRAEL looks at her. STEFA touches his face and holds it in her hands. Then she exits into the girls' dormitory.*

(off stage, to SARA) Sara, put that away . . .

SARA: *(off)* Stefa!

STEFA: *(off)* Right now, and get back into your bed.

SARA: *(off)* Stefa . . . !

> *METTYE puts her arms around ISRAEL and kisses him.*

> *Transition.*

Scene Eleven.

Now METTYE *has her arms around* SARA.

KORCZAK *and* STEFA *stand behind them.*

It's evening, before curfew but after nightfall (the time of day when it's possible to escape the ghetto).

There is no suitcase.

SARA *pulls on* METTYE *as if she's going to bolt back into the orphanage.* METTYE *holds her and physically restrains her, keeps her from going back inside.*

METTYE: Sara.

SARA *is hyperventilating.*

Sara, stop it—

SARA, *hyperventilating, continues under.*

SARA: No.

METTYE: Listen to me—listen—you're going to go and play the violin—Sara!

SARA: No.

METTYE: *(sharp)* You're going to—stop it! You're going to go and play concerts—

SARA: *(as in "I don't want to go")* No.

METTYE: Yes, you are. You can't play only for me—I don't even like the violin that much—well I don't—Sara, stop it! You have to go—you have to go now—

SARA tries to get away from her.

SARA: No.

METTYE holds her.

METTYE: Say goodbye to me.

The girls stand together, look at each other. Then STEFA starts to pull on SARA's arm and walk her away.

SARA: *(to STEFA)* No, no! I want to tell her something!

METTYE: What.

Beat.

What.

SARA: I'm sorry.

METTYE: It's all right: you go. I want you to: we'll meet . . . somewhere else.

The girls stand together for a moment.

Then STEFA *pulls* SARA *out of* METTYE'S *arms.*

STEFA *and* SARA *exit quickly,* STEFA *pulling* SARA *off through the courtyard gateway.*

She's gone.

KORCZAK: Yes.

Transition.

Intermezzo Six.

The PERFORMER PLAYING METTYE turns out to the audience and speaks into a microphone.

PERFORMER PLAYING METTYE: *(to audience)* Sara hides in Warsaw for three years. After the war, she trains in Paris. She plays first with the Paris Orchestra, and then all over the world. She gets married. She has a little boy and a little girl. She loves Mettye all her life, and in 2003, when she's dying, she sees a bird come and land on her hospital bed. It's the last thing she sees before she closes her eyes.

During the above, the PERFORMER PLAYING SARA comes on stage holding a lit candle. Now she blows it out.

Transition.

Scene Twelve.

KORCZAK is in his office, scribbling in his journal.

The vodka bottle, now only half full, sits in front of him.

ISRAEL appears in the doorway.

KORCZAK: You're awake.

ISRAEL: Yeah.

KORCZAK: Why?

ISRAEL shrugs.

ISRAEL: Why are you awake?

KORCZAK shrugs in return.

KORCZAK: What do you need? Some water?

ISRAEL: No. Can I have a little vodka?

KORCZAK hands ISRAEL the bottle. ISRAEL drinks.

KORCZAK: You can't sleep?

ISRAEL: No.

KORCZAK: Are you scared?

ISRAEL: Are you?

KORCZAK: I am, yeah.

ISRAEL: Of what?

Beat.

KORCZAK: I'm scared of . . .

Beat.

Of talking to the children about . . . dying.

Beat.

ISRAEL: Yeah?

Beat.

My father said to me that . . . it's easy. He said it didn't hurt: it was like a light was shining on him. He said I shouldn't worry, it's just . . . closing your eyes.

KORCZAK: Why did he tell you that? You were sick too?

ISRAEL: Yeah. They . . . took me to the graveyard.

KORCZAK: What do you mean: "they took you"?

ISRAEL: I was sick and . . . not moving.

KORCZAK: They . . . ? They thought you were *dead?*

ISRAEL nods.

ISRAEL: They put dirt on me then . . . I sat up. My father was there—in the hole. I was coughing so they pulled me out. Then they walked me to the street and left me.

Beat.

KORCZAK: Did it comfort you, what your father said?

ISRAEL nods.

A light shining on you . . . ?

ISRAEL: Yeah. I think about it when . . .

ISRAEL points at the vodka.

Can I have more of the . . . ?

KORCZAK: Have it.

KORCZAK passes the vodka back to him. ISRAEL drinks.

ISRAEL: We're going to the East.

KORCZAK: All of us, yes: they're evacuating the ghetto, to work camps, they say, but I . . . I don't think the children will . . . I don't think the East is . . .

Beat.

ISRAEL: Yeah.

Beat.

ISRAEL: When the orphanage?

KORCZAK: Any time now . . .

Beat.

They're smuggling in weapons?

ISRAEL nods.

ISRAEL: Yeah.

KORCZAK: Israel, you should go, and . . . fight with them. Or you should run. Try and get out. You know how to get through. You should go into Warsaw, hide . . .

ISRAEL: They'd catch me.

KORCZAK: There's a chance they won't.

ISRAEL: No, there's not. Or . . . not enough of one.

Beat.

I'll . . . stay, with you.

Beat.

(low) Don't be scared.

ISRAEL takes KORCZAK's hands in his and rubs them.

Transition.

Intermezzo Seven.

ISRAEL slowly walks downstage and turns to the audience for the first time.

He walks right up to the edge, as close to the audience as he can. He holds a microphone.

PERFORMER PLAYING ISRAEL: *(to audience)* A few days later, the Gestapo come.

And then we hear heavy banging at the door, the sound made by all the performers banging microphones against the floor.

They have dogs and machine guns.

We hear the banging again, louder.

The smallest children hold one thing in their hands: a doll or a photograph of their family. Something to comfort them. Everyone else carries something too—a bag or . . . gives you something to . . . hold.

We hear the banging again, ominous, louder.

But the Germans are . . .

ISRAEL shrugs.

Beat.

It's hard not to be . . . scared, even if . . . if . . .

We hear the banging again, escalating, escalating, deafening.

The sound is so loud that the PERFORMER PLAYING ISRAEL *is blinking, cringing, covering his ears.*

Transition.

Scene Thirteen.

All the performers except SARA *huddle around* ISRAEL *at the edge of the stage. There is a constant, distant sound of banging on the door, muted, as though we're underwater.*

Meanwhile, at the back of the stage, the PERFORMER PLAYING SARA *draws a sun on the wall with chalk.*

KORCZAK: I'd like to go for a walk. Where should we walk?

Beat.

METTYE: Kraków?

KORCZAK: We could walk to Kraków. But no, I was thinking of some-where further. I was thinking we should go to the sun.

MISHA: The sun.

KORCZAK: It's a long walk, but I think we can do it. Israel can tell us which streets to take, and once we get out of the city, Mettye, you can ask the birds if we're walking in the right direction. And Misha, you could read to us, in the evenings, from the Torah: we'll be bored but we'll pretend to like it. And Stefa will keep the little ones from lagging too far behind. And we'll walk and walk until we get to the sun. We'll know we're there because it'll be very bright. What do you think? Shall we go to the sun?

The PERFORMER PLAYING SARA turns to the audience and speaks into a microphone.

PERFORMER PLAYING SARA: *(to audience)* A bright light shines on them all. The light is intensely bright.

As the PERFORMER PLAYING SARA has said, the light is intensely bright.

A "bright-out."

(to the audience) Blackout.

The lights flick out: death.

End play.

Afterword
Amanda West Lewis

I had never heard of Janusz Korczak until 2005, when I met Leon Gluzman. Leon owned a building in Ottawa that became the home of the Ottawa School of Speech and Drama (OSSD), a non-profit theatre school for children and youth of which I was Artistic Director. Leon was excited by the work OSSD was doing—not because he had any interest in theatre, but because he loved watching the children.

Leon told me the story of his own childhood in Poland after the First World War. His father had died suddenly when he was six years old, and his mother and sisters had to go out to work in a laundry to support the family. With no money, and no one to look after him, Leon ended up in one of Korczak's orphanages.

Leon's ninety-two-year-old eyes shone when he told me about "Pan Doktor." He became a child again. He told me about the Children's Court, Korczak's teasing sense of humour, and the stories Korczak wrote. But most importantly, Leon talked about what it felt like to be shown respect. He introduced me to the man who is known in Jewish tradition as one of the Thirty-Six Just Men—someone with a pure soul who makes possible the world's salvation. Through Leon, I got to know Korczak from a very personal, child-like perspective.

Leon became OSSD's main benefactor, and we wanted to honour his support. We could think of no more fitting tribute than to create a play about Janusz Korczak. Given the subject, we thought that it was fundamental for our project to be child centred. So in 2007 we decided to hold a week-long workshop with ten youth actors, ten to fourteen years old, guided by a team of theatre professionals.

In that first workshop, the young people interviewed Leon and researched Korczak's life. They improvised scenes, wrote bits of text, and explored movement and music of the period. They sought out the heart of Korczak's teachings and showed us what resonated with them.

As we worked with these young people, we realized that we needed a skilled playwright to develop our ideas beyond the workshop phase. I discussed the project with Lise Ann Johnson at the Great Canadian Theatre Company (GCTC), and we were thrilled when Hannah Moscovitch agreed to work with us.

We conducted subsequent workshops in which the young people were equal members of the professional team. Given the subject matter, it was often painful work. But we were all bolstered by Korczak's humanity, by Leon's delight, and by the children's willingness to explore hard concepts.

The Children's Republic has evolved far beyond our humble beginnings. But I think its power comes from having had children involved at its inception. The play explores themes and questions that became apparent to us in those early workshops: What are the roots of anger and brutality in a child? Can we forgive injustice? What is freedom? And perhaps, most importantly, how can we give children light when the darkness descends?

In *The Children's Republic*, the children help us find answers. The answers start small because they are child-sized, but we know that from one small person ripples can move outward through time and space. When I met Leon Gluzman, it was the child in him who introduced me to Janusz Korczak. Leon sent the ripples begun by Korczak into our small project. Hannah Moscovitch, with her skill, grace, and wisdom, has moved those ripples outward into the larger world.

I have no doubt that everyone who travels along this journey with Israel, Misha, Mettye, Sara, Korczak, and Stefa will continue to send those ripples outward and make a difference.

Amanda West Lewis has built a life filled with words on the page and on the stage, combining careers as a writer, theatre director, and calligrapher. She is the artistic director and founder of the Ottawa Children's Theatre, a company dedicated to enriching young lives through drama. Amanda holds an M.F.A. in Writing for Children and Young Adults from the Vermont College of Fine Arts, with a specialist certificate in writing picture books. Her published work includes seven books for children and youth ranging from historical YA fiction to craft and picture books. A professional calligrapher, her work has been featured in international shows and she has taught the history of letterform throughout Ontario. She is passionate about the importance of arts education for all ages. You can find more about Amanda at http://www.amandawestlewis.com, on Facebook at @amandawest.lewis, and on Twitter at @AmandaWestLewis.

Acknowledgements

I'd like to acknowledge, first of all, Leon Gluzman, who was a child in Janusz Korczak's orphanage, and who inspired this project. Huge thanks are due to Amanda Lewis, Lise Ann Johnson, Richard Rose, David Eisner, and Avery Saltzman for developing and producing the play. I am so very grateful to Michael Shamata at the Belfry Theatre for allowing me to rethink the play for a third time. It meant I could finally write the play the way I had dreamed it all along (but had been lacking the skill to realize it).

I'd like to acknowledge the following works: *The Warsaw Ghetto: A Guide to the Perished City* by Barbara Engelking and Jacek Leociak; *Notes from the Warsaw Ghetto* by Emmanuel Ringelblum; *The King of Children: The Life and Death of Janus Korczak* by Betty Jean Lifton; *Father of the Orphans: The Story of Janusz Korczak* by Mark Bernheim; *When I am Little Again* and *The Child's Right to Respect* by Janusz Korczak, translated by E.P. Kulawiec; *King Matt the First* by Janusz Korczak, translated by Jerzy Srokowski; and *Ghetto Diary* by Janusz Korczak, with an introduction by Betty Jean Lifton.

Hannah Moscovitch is an acclaimed Canadian playwright, TV writer, and librettist whose work has been widely produced in Canada and around the world. Recent stage work includes *Sexual Misconduct of the Middle Classes* and *Old Stock: A Refugee Love Story* (co-created with Christian Barry and Ben Caplan). Hannah has been the recipient of numerous awards, including the Governor General's Literary Award, the Trillium Book Award, the Nova Scotia Masterworks Arts Award, the Scotsman Fringe First and the Herald Angel Awards at the Edinburgh Festival Fringe, and the prestigious Windham-Campbell Prize administered by Yale University. She has been nominated for the international Susan Smith Blackburn Prize, the Drama Desk Award, and Canada's Siminovitch Prize in Theatre. She is a playwright-in-residence at Tarragon Theatre in Toronto. She lives in Halifax.

First edition: February 2022
Printed and bound in Canada by Imprimerie Gauvin, Gatineau

Jacket design by Monnet Design
Author photo © Alejandro Santiago

PLAYWRIGHTS
CANADA PRESS

202-269 Richmond St. w.
Toronto, ON
M5V 1X1

416.703.0013
info@playwrightscanada.com
www.playwrightscanada.com
@playcanpress

MIX
Paper
FSC® C100212